INCLINED PLANES

Author: David and Patricia Armentrout

ROURKE PUBLISHING

Vero Beach, Florida 32964

www.rourkepublishing.com

PHOTO CREDITS: Title pg © Lugo; pg 04 © Armentrout; pg 5 © Ian Wilson; pg 6 © Fred Sweet; pg 07 © Armentrout; pg 10-11 © Thomas Hansson; pg 12-13 © Morozova Oksana; pg 14-15 © Armentrout; pg 16 © Michelle Donahue Hillison; pg 17 © Kameel4u; pg 18 © Orange Line Media; pg 19 © Robert J. Beyers II; pg 20-21 © clearviewstock; pg 22a © Vladimir Ivanovich Danilov; pg 22b © Jacek Chabraszewski

Edited by Kelli Hicks

Cover and Interior designed by Tara Raymo

Library of Congress Cataloging-in-Publication Data

Cover Armentrout, David, 1962-
  Inclined planes / David and Patricia Armentrout.
    p. cm. -- (Simple machines)
  Previous ed. by Patricia Armentrout under title: Inclined plane.
  ISBN 978-1-60694-387-8   hardcover
  ISBN 978-1-60694-519-3   softcover
  1. Inclined planes--Juvenile literature. I. Armentrout, Patricia, 1960- II.
Armentrout, Patricia, 1960- Inclined plane. III. Title.
  TJ147.A76 2010
  621.8--dc22

                        2009006069

www.rourkepublishing.com – rourke@rourkepublishing.com
Post Office Box 643328 Vero Beach, Florida 32964

TABLE OF CONTENTS

DOING WORK WITH LESS EFFORT

What comes to mind when you hear the word machine? Do you imagine a shiny, red racecar speeding around a track? Maybe you picture a farmer on a muddy tractor plowing a farmer's field. Or, you might see a dishwasher, and remember you are supposed to unload it!

The dishwasher does the cleaning, but you still have to unload it.

It doesn't matter if it is a car, tractor, dishwasher, or something as simple as a ramp; it is a machine if it helps you do work with less **effort**.

SIMPLE MACHINES

We use racecars, tractors, and dishwashers for different purposes. However, they are all machines. In fact, they are **complex machines** because they have many moving parts. Some parts of complex machines are machines themselves, called simple machines.

The wheel, lever, pulley, screw, wedge, and inclined plane are simple machines. Simple machines have very few, if any, moving parts.

Parts of a complex machine engine are held together with simple machines like screws.

INCLINED PLANE

An inclined plane is a slanted surface. It may seem too simple to be a machine, but a slanted surface can make our work easier.

Picture a ramp at the rear of a delivery truck. The ramp is an inclined plane. It connects a high surface to a low surface. We use it to move objects into and out of the truck. Why use the ramp? Because, it's easier to move heavy objects down the ramp than to lower them from the truck to the ground.

Without a ramp, it might take two workers to load or unload a heavy object.

LESS EFFORT OVER A GREATER DISTANCE

Can an inclined plane help you do more work? No, an inclined plane allows you to do the same amount of work, but with less effort.

Imagine climbing a steep hill. Going straight up is the shortest route. But, it is also the most difficult way to get to the top. What if there was a trail that circled up the hill? If you followed a **gradual slope** up the hill, it would be an easier climb. In the end, you climbed the same hill, and completed the same work.

It's fun to climb straight up a mountain, but it takes a lot of effort.

When you use an inclined plane, you trade effort for distance. Taking the gradual slope around the hill is easier, but takes longer. When you apply less effort over a greater distance, you gain a **mechanical advantage**.

A gradual climb to the top gives you time to enjoy the view.

GRAVITY AND INCLINED PLANES

Gravity is a force that pulls objects toward the ground. You can build an inclined plane. See how gravity and inclined planes work together.

You need a stiff board, a stack of books, and a toy car. Stack the books. Lay the board flat along side the books. Set your car on the board. What happens? Nothing. The flat surface did not affect the movement of the car, (even though it has wheels for rolling). Next, lean one edge of the board against the top of the books to form a slope. Set the car near the top of the slope and let go. What happens? Does gravity pull the car down the slope?

Without gravity, inclined planes would not be as useful.

COMMON INCLINED PLANES

A staircase may be the most common inclined plane we use. A staircase connects different levels. If we didn't have a staircase, we would need a ladder. Picture a ladder standing up connecting a lower level to an upper level. Now imagine a staircase connecting the same two levels. The stairs use more space. You have to travel a greater distance to get where you're going, but stairs sure make the job easier!

A staircase allows us to use less effort to get from one level to the next.

Look at the buildings and homes in your community. Many of them probably have sloped roofs. Why do we use inclined planes in building construction? They are common because gravity allows rain and snow to easily slide off sloped roofs.

Next time you go by a construction site, look at the heavy equipment. Do you see any inclined planes? Watch the cement trucks. They have a sloping chute at the rear for wet cement to flow. Watch the dump trucks. Their load pours down an inclined plane when drivers raise one end of the bed.

Imagine how hard it would be to unload this dirt without the inclined plane.

PLAYING WITH INCLINED PLANES

Inclined planes help us do work with less effort, but we use them for fun, too! Maybe you have spent time at a park or school playground. Did you climb to the top of the slide and let gravity carry you to the bottom? Have you ever been to a water park on a hot summer day? Most likely, you waited a long time to ride down a slippery slide.

Who knew a simple machine could be this much fun?

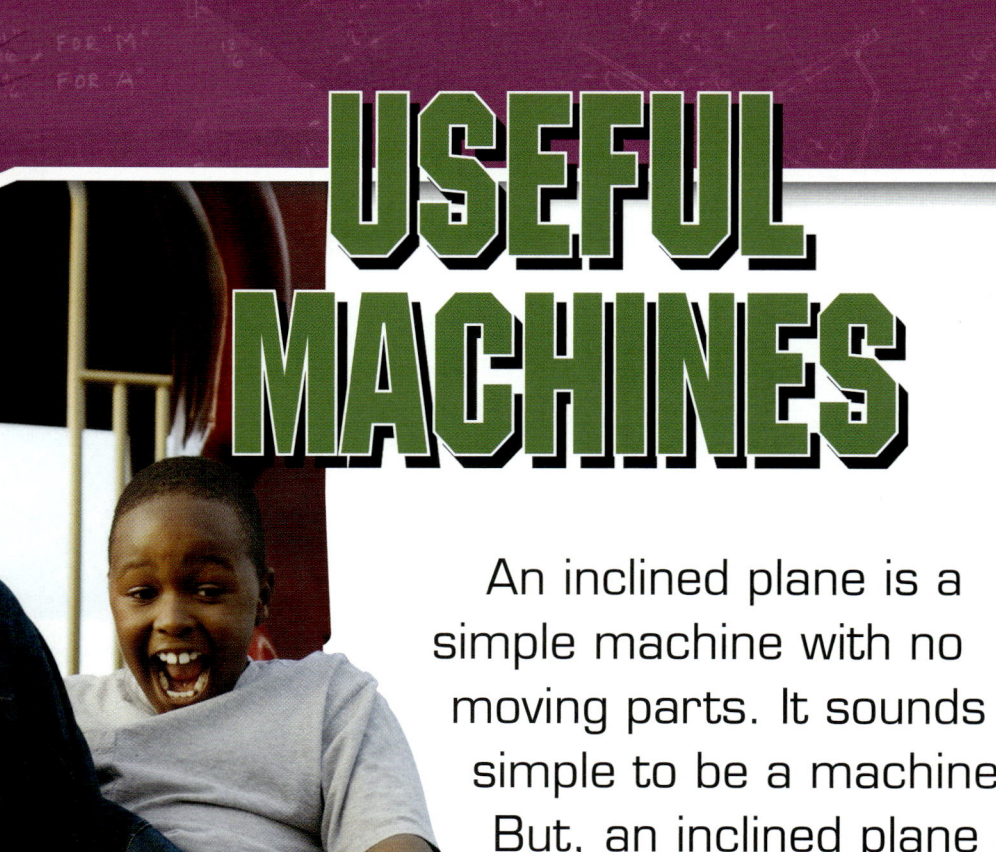

USEFUL MACHINES

An inclined plane is a simple machine with no moving parts. It sounds too simple to be a machine. But, an inclined plane can make your work easier. Whether you are indoors or outside, working or playing, inclined planes are useful, simple machines.

It's true inclined planes make our work easier, but who wants to think about work?

GLOSSARY

complex machines (KAHM-pleks muh-SHEENZ): machines with many moving parts

effort (EF-urt): force used to move or lift a weight or an object

gradual slope (GRAJ-yoo-uhl SLOHP): a slowly progressing angle that is easy to walk or climb

gravity (GRAV-uh-tee): an invisible force that pulls things down toward the Earth's center

mechanical advantage (mi-KAN-eh-kul ad-VAN-tij): what you gain when a simple machine allows you to use less effort

INDEX

WEBSITES TO VISIT

www.kidskonnect.com/content/view/99/27/
www.edheads.org/activities/simple-machines/
www.brainpop.com/technology/simplemachines/

ABOUT THE AUTHORS

David and Patricia Armentrout specialize in nonfiction children's books. They enjoy exploring different topics, and have written on a variety of subjects, including communities, sports, animals, and people. David and Patricia love to spend their free time outdoors with their two boys and dog Max.